GIFTED & TALENTED®

*To develop
your child's gifts
and talents*

READING

GIFTED
&
TALENTED®

*To develop
your child's gifts
and talents*

READING

A Workbook for Ages 4–6

Written by Susan Amerikaner • Illustrated by Leesa Whitten

Lowell House House
Juvenile
Los Angeles
CONTEMPORARY
BOOKS
Chicago

ISBN 0-929923-83-9

10 9 8 7 6 5

Cover design: Brenda Leach
Cover illustration: Dave Lowe

GIFTED AND TALENTED WORKBOOKS will help develop your child's natural talents and gifts by providing activities to enhance critical and creative thinking skills. These skills of logic and reasoning teach children **how** to think. They are precisely the skills emphasized by teachers of gifted and talented children.

Thinking skills are the skills needed to be able to learn anything at any time. Unlike events, words, and teaching methods, thinking skills never change. If a child has a grasp of how to think, school success and even success in life will become more assured. In addition, the child will become self-confident as he or she approaches new tasks with the ability to think them through and discover solutions.

GIFTED AND TALENTED WORKBOOKS present these skills in a unique way, combining the basic subject areas of reading, language arts, and math with thinking skills. The top of each page is labeled to indicate the specific thinking skill developed. Here are some of the skills you will find:

- Deduction – the ability to reach a logical conclusion by interpreting clues

- Understanding Relationships – the ability to recognize how objects, shapes, and words are similar or dissimilar; to classify and categorize

- Sequencing – the ability to organize events, numbers; to recognize patterns

- Inference – the ability to reach logical conclusions from given or assumed evidence

- Creative Thinking – the ability to generate unique ideas; to compare and contrast the same elements in different situations; to present imaginative solutions to problems

How to Use Gifted & Talented Workbooks

Each book contains activities that challenge children. The activities vary in range from easier to more difficult. You may need to work with your child on many of the pages, especially with the child who is a non-reader. However, even a non-reader can master thinking skills, and the sooner your child learns how to think, the better. Read the directions to your child, and if necessary, explain them. Let your child choose to do the activities that interest him or her. When interest wanes, stop. A page or two at a time may be enough, as the child should have fun while learning.

It is important to remember that these activities are designed to teach your child **how to think,** not how to find the right answer. Teachers of gifted children are never surprised when a child discovers a new "right" answer. For example, a child may be asked to choose the object that doesn't belong in this group: a table, a chair, a book, a desk. The best answer is **book,** since all the others are furniture. But a child could respond that all of them belong because they all could be found in an office. The best way to react to this type of response is to praise the child and gently point out that there is another answer too. While creativity should be encouraged, your child must look for the best and most **suitable** answer.

GIFTED AND TALENTED WORKBOOKS have been written and designed by teachers. Educationally sound and endorsed by leaders in the gifted field, this series will benefit any child who demonstrates curiosity, imagination, a sense of fun and wonder about the world, and a desire to learn. These books will open your child's mind to new experiences and help fulfill his or her true potential.

Color the 's.

1. The blue one is on top.

2. The yellow one is on the bottom.

3. One is green.

Color the 's.

1. The yellow one is on the bottom.

2. The blue one is under the orange one.

Draw a line to put each animal in its cage.

1. The **lion** goes on the bottom.

2. The **monkey** goes in the middle.

3. Where does the **tiger** go?

lion

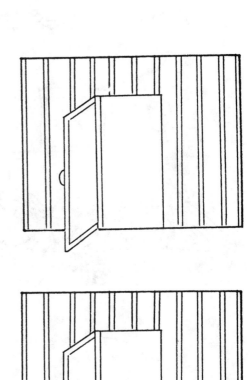

tiger

monkey

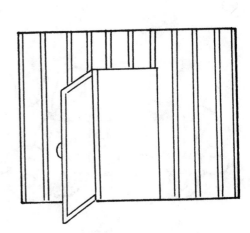

Draw a line to put each toy where it belongs.

1. The **car** goes on top.

2. The **ball** does **not** go in the middle.

3. Where does the **train** go?

train

ball

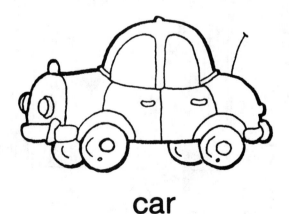

car

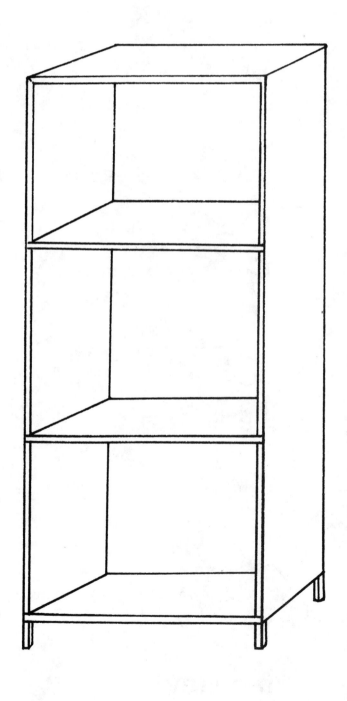

Color the  .

1. The bottom is strawberry.

2. Chocolate is under the orange.

Color the  's.

1. The blue one is first.

2. The yellow one is behind the red one.

Color the  's.

1. The is on top.

2. The is on the bottom.

3. The 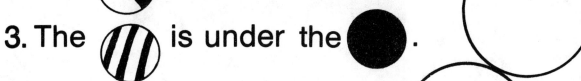 is under the .

Color the 's.

1. The blue one is last.

2. The yellow one is in front of the red one.

Color the  's.

1. The blue one is first.

2. The green one is **not** next to the blue one.

3. **Where is the red bear?**

Color the 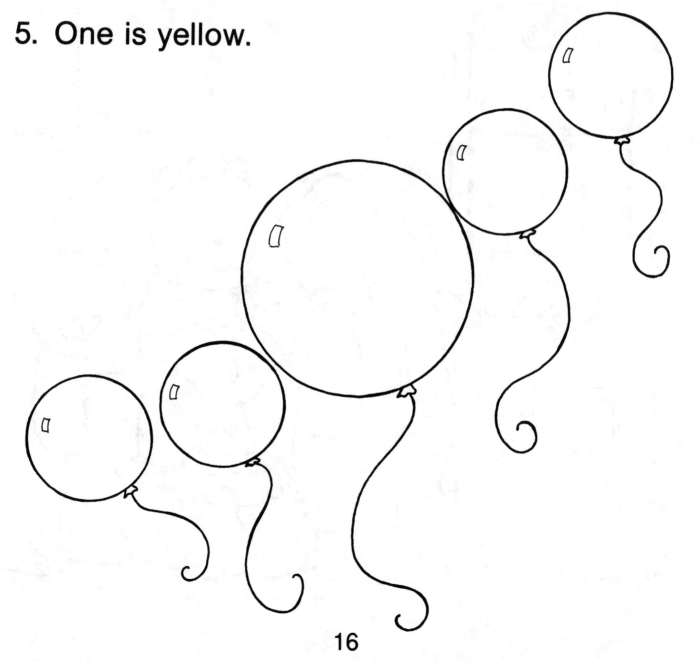 's.

1. The big one is red.

2. The orange one is highest.

3. The blue one is between the red and orange ones.

4. The green one is **not** next to the red one.

5. One is yellow.

16

Which animal is this?

Color the animal you see in the puzzle:

Note: On these "puzzle" pages, your child may want to cut out the pieces and fit them together to check the answer.

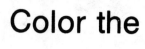

Color the line yellow.

Color the line purple.

18

Who is this?

Color the face you see in the puzzle :

Color the  line yellow.

Color the line black.

Color the line orange.

Which animal is this?

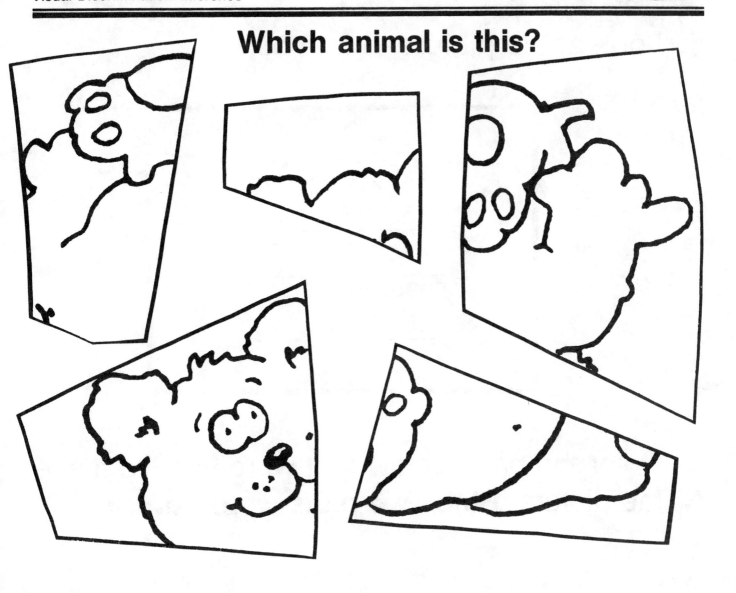

Color the animal you see in the puzzle :

1. Look at the picture in this box:

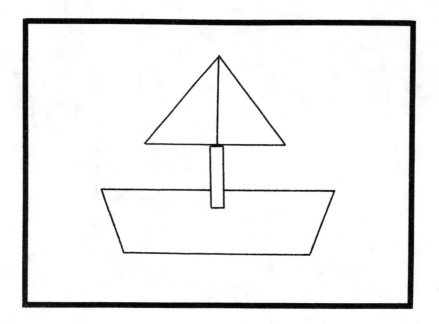

2. Color the parts below that were used to make the picture. **Hint:** Two parts were **not** used!

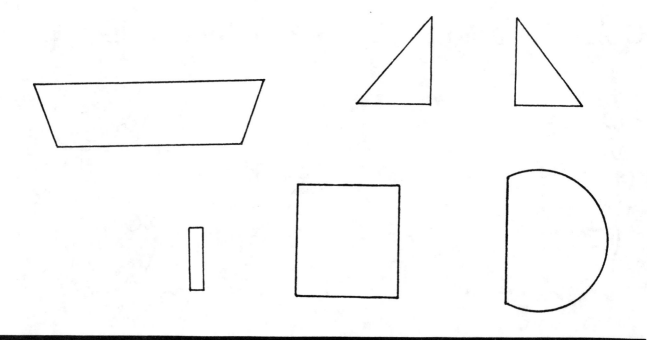

What is it?

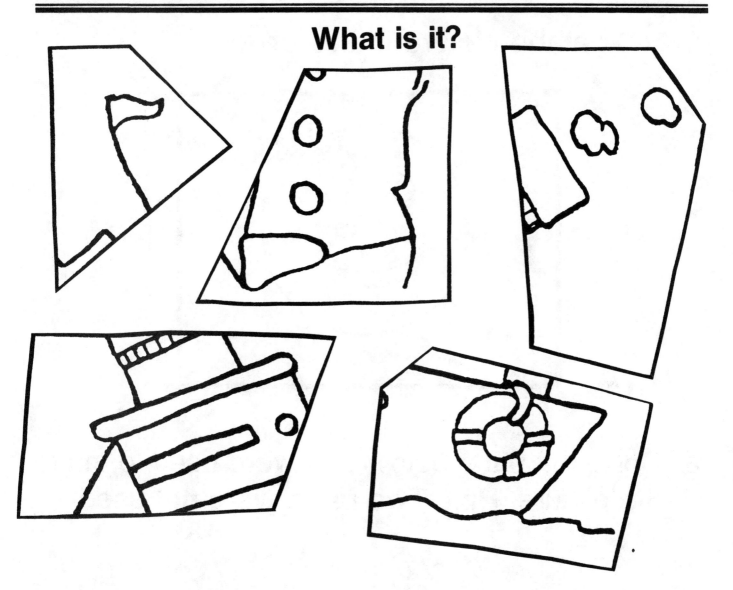

Color the object you see in the puzzle:

1. Look at the picture in this box:

2. Color the parts below that were used to make the picture. **Hint:** Two parts were **not** used!

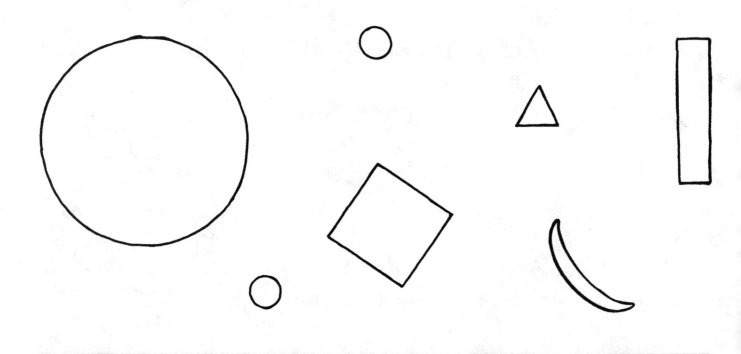

Draw a line from the pieces to the things they make when they are put together.

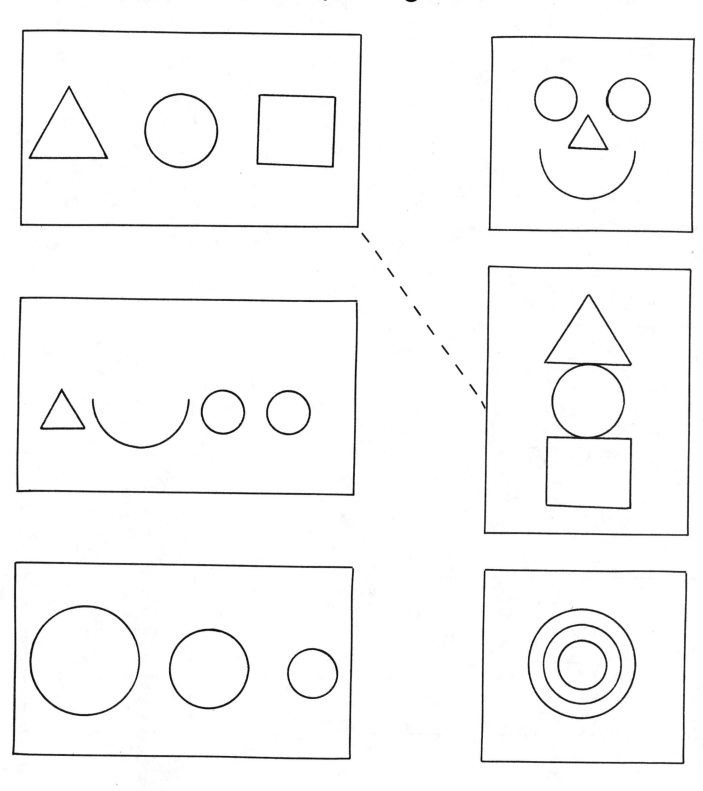

Draw a line from the pieces to the things they make when they are put together.

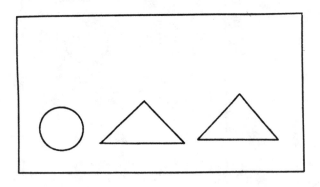

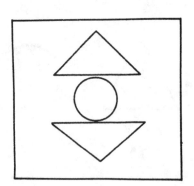

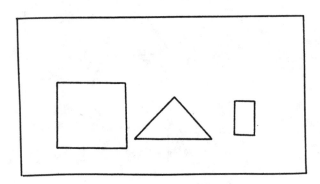

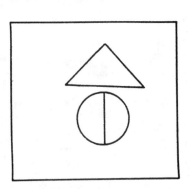

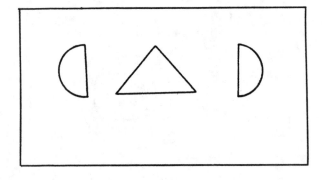

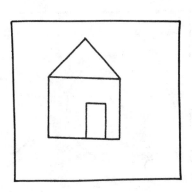

Draw a line to show what you can make.

Draw a line to show where these things belong.

Draw a line from the objects to the people who use them.

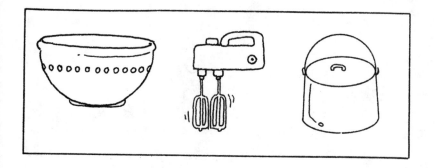

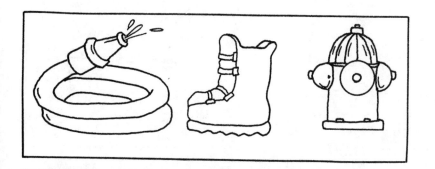

Draw a line from the people to the things they see.

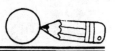

Circle the three things in each row that go together.

You use them to clean.

You use them to eat.

   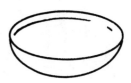

You use them to ride.

You use them to fix things.

You use them to make music.

Circle the three pictures in each row that go together.

You go to a museum to look at these:

  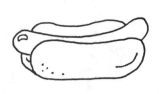 

You use them to get a closer look.

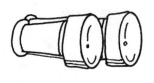  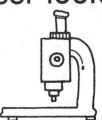 

You sit on them.

You find them at a party.

You find them in fairy tales.

Circle the three things in each row that go together.

They have fur.

They are made of metal.

They live in the desert.

They are alive.

They are heavy.

Put an X on the one thing in each row that does **not** belong.

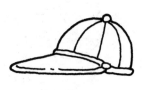   

Put an X on the one thing in each row that does **not** belong.

Put an X on the one thing in each row that does **not** belong.

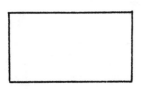  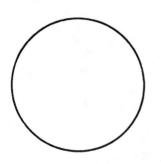 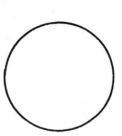 

 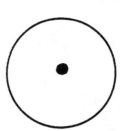 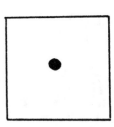

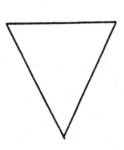 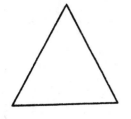 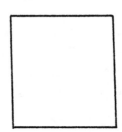 

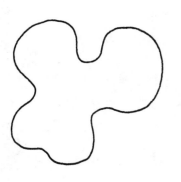 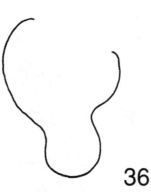  

Draw one more picture that goes with the things in each box.

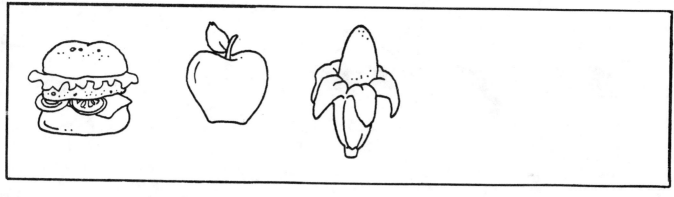

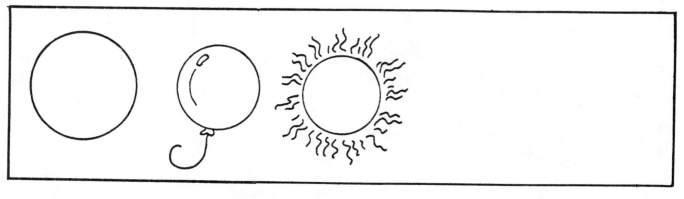

Draw one more picture that goes with the things in each box.

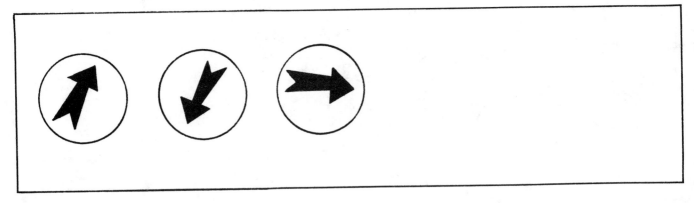

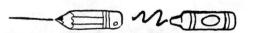

Draw a line to the box that shows the missing part of the story. Color the story.

1 **2** **3**

1 **2** **3**

Draw a line to the box that shows the missing part of the story. Color the story.

1 **2** **3**

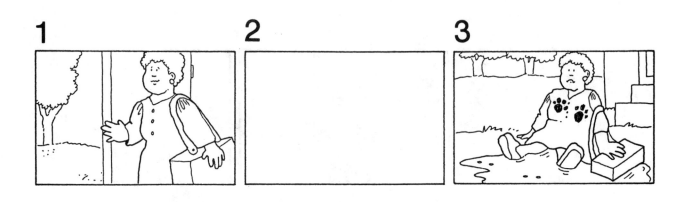

1 **2** **3**

Draw a line to the box that shows the missing part of the story. Color the story.

1  **2** 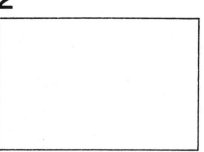 **3**

1  **2** 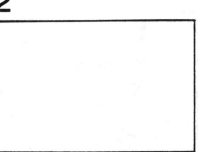 **3**

41

Draw a line to the box that shows the missing part of the story. Color the story.

1   **2**   **3**

1   **2**   **3**

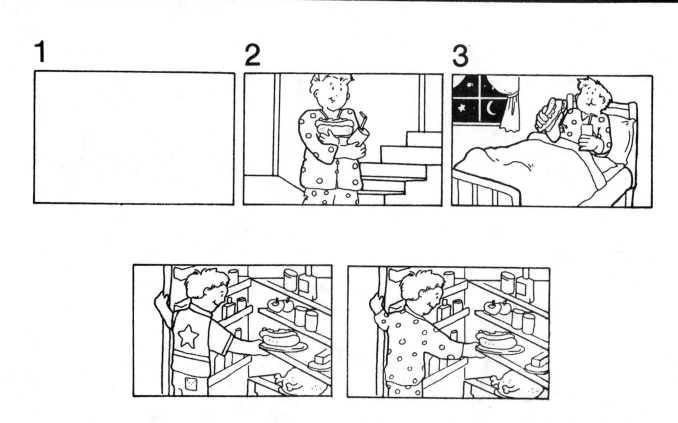

Draw a line to the box that shows the missing part of the story. Color the story.

1   **2**   **3**

1   **2**   **3**

 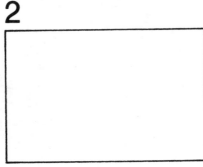 

Look at all the pictures, one at a time. When you think you can remember them all, look at the next page.

Find the pictures you saw on the page before. Circle **only** the pictures you saw before.

Now look back and check. Did you remember them all?

Look at all the pictures, one at a time. When you think you can remember them all, look at the next page.

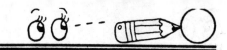

Find the pictures you saw on the page before. Circle **only** the pictures you saw before.

Now look back and check. Did you remember them all?

Look at all the pictures, one at a time. When you think you can remember them all, look at the next page.

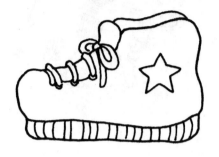

Find the pictures you saw on the page before. Circle **only** the pictures you saw before.

Now look back and check. Did you remember them all?

Look at all the pictures, one at a time. When you think you can remember them all, look at the next page.

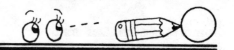

Find the pictures you saw on the page before. Circle **only** the pictures you saw before.

Now look back and check. Did you remember them all?

Which clown is Howdy Clown?

1. Read all about Howdy.   2. Color Howdy.

Howdy is **not** fat.

Howdy has a hat.

Howdy is happy.

Which dog is Rover?

1. Read all about Rover.   2. Color Rover.

Rover is big.

Rover does **not** have spots.

Rover has a long tail.

Which boy is Mike?

1. Read all about Mike.   2. Color Mike.

Mike likes to play ball.

Mike is tall.

Mike does **not** have a hat.

Mike is happy.

Which pirate is Long John?

1. Read all about Long John. 2. Color Long John.

Long John has one leg.

Long John has a hat.

Long John has a bird.

Long John is **not** happy.

Which picture is Amy's picture?

1. Read all about Amy's picture. 2. Color it.

Amy's picture has a tree.

It does **not** have a house.

It has two girls and one dog.

Which room is Jon's room?

1. Read all about Jon's room.   2. Color it.

One shoe is on the floor.

His teddy bear is on the bed.

He forgot to make his bed today.

Which monster is on T.V.?

1. Read all about the T.V. monster.   2. Color it.

It has more than two eyes.

It has a long neck.

It does **not** have teeth.

What does Nina see?

1. Read all about what she sees.   Color it.

It does **not** have spots.

It does **not** have wings.

It is long.

It has more than six legs.

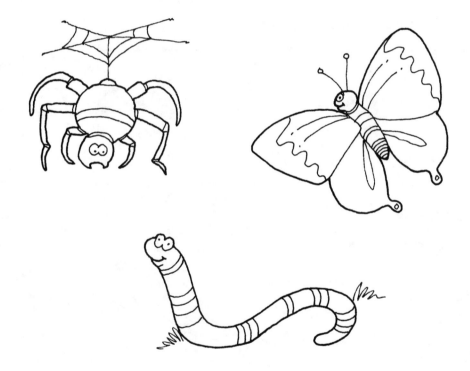

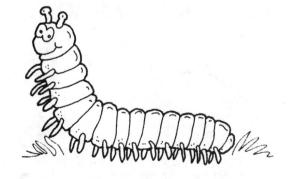

Put an X on the one thing in each row that you do **not** need.

To make pizza:

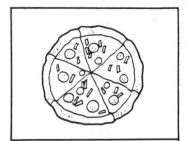 

To make a garden:

To make a doghouse:

To make a sandwich:

Put an X on the one thing in each row that you do **not** need.

To send a letter:

To make pancakes:

To wash a car:

To get dressed:

Put an X on the one thing in each row that you do **not** need.

To play baseball:

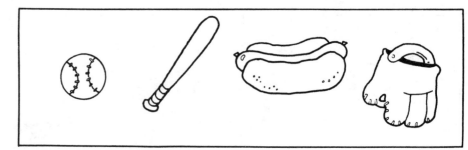

To have a picnic:

To go fishing:

To brush your teeth:

Make the pictures in each row look the same. Fill in the missing parts.

Make the pictures in each row look the same. Fill in the missing parts.

What do you see?

1. Circle the picture below that shows what you **see**.
2. Fill in the missing parts of the picture.

What do you see?

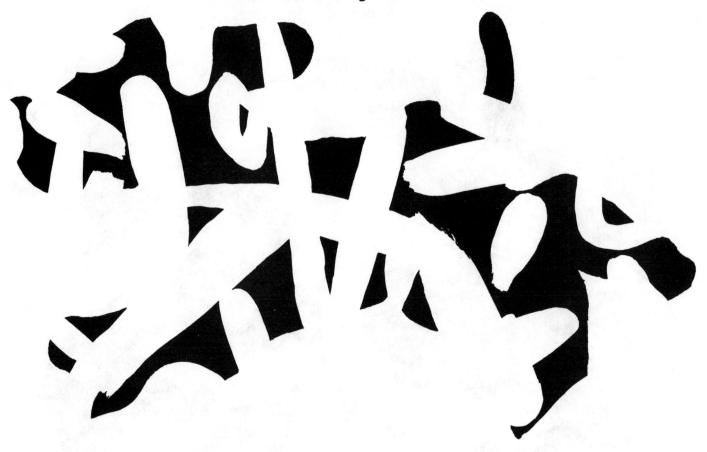

1. Circle the picture below that shows what you see.

2. Fill in the missing parts of the picture.

1. Draw a line to the pictures that will look the same when the missing parts are filled in.
2. Fill in the missing parts.

1. Draw a line to the pictures that will look the same when the missing parts are filled in.

2. Fill in the missing parts.

Draw a line to show which pictures are exactly the same.

Draw a line to show which pictures are exactly the same.

Draw a line to show which pictures are exactly the same.

71

Circle the picture in each row that is the same as the one in the box — **but turned in a different way.**

Circle the picture in each row that is the same as the one in the box — **but turned in a different way.**

Circle the picture in each row that is the same as the one in the box — **but turned in a different way.**

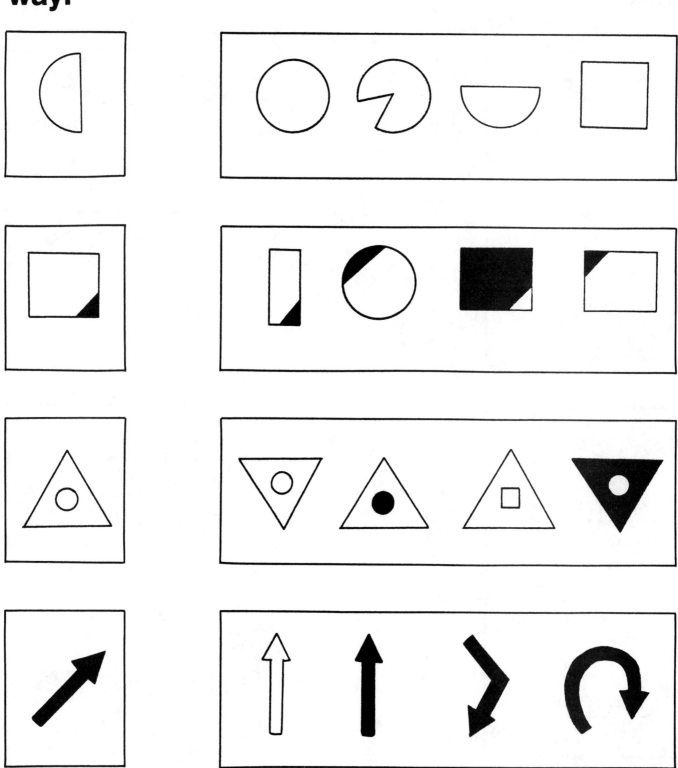

Circle the picture in each row that is the same as the one in the box — **but turned in a different way.**

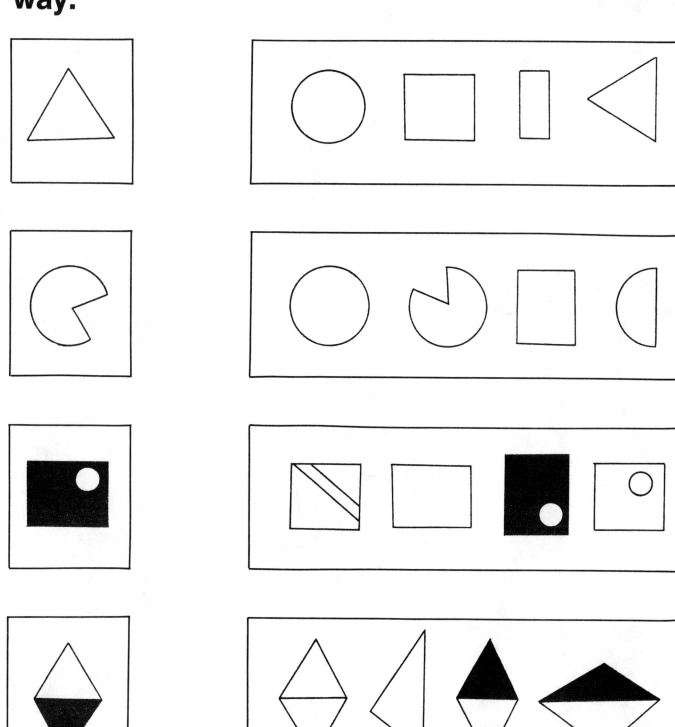

Find and color the two clowns that are the same as the one in the box — **but turned in different positions.**

Find and color the two monsters that are the same as the one in the box — **but turned in different positions.**

Find and color the two dogs that are the same as the one in the box — **but turned in different positions.**

Circle the three letters in each row that are same as the one in the box.

Hint:
The letters may be upside down, backwards, or sideways!

| a | a ɐ o ʊ a |

| e | ɯ e ⊆ ɯ u |

| h | ρ ⅃ ɥ u ɥ |

| r | ˥ r ʊ ɹ n |

Circle the three words in each row that are the same as the one in the box.

Hint:
The word may be upside down, backwards, or sideways!

cat	tac ʇɐɔ cᵤₚ t aᶜ

big	bug ɓıq gᵢᵇ gib

go	og on ɓo go

yes	ˢeᵧ ˢaᵧ səʎ ˢếʎ

80

Color the four cars with the same word as the one in the box.

Hint:
The word may be sideways, upside down, or backwards!

car

Color the four balls with the same word as the one in the box.

ball

Hint:

The word may be sideways, upside down, or backwards!

Color the four houses with the same word as the one in the box.

house

Hint:

The word may be sideways, upside down, or backwards!

Color the **one** picture in each row that both words best describe.

Tall and thin

Short and fat

Tall and fat

Short and thin

Color the **one** picture in each row that both words best describe.

Sweet and cold

Sweet and sticky

 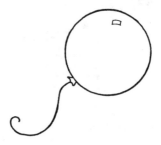 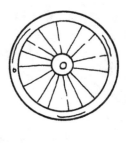

Round and light

Little and soft

Color the **one** picture in each row that both words best describe.

Sweet and juicy

Hot and far away

Small and sharp

Big and alive

In each box, draw a picture that fits the words.

Red and sweet

Tall and alive

Happy and alive

Big and furry

Blue and square

Big and scary

Circle the picture that best completes the sentence.

 **is to**  **as** 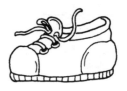 **is to**

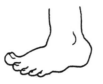

 **is to**  **as**  **is to**

 **is to** 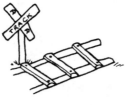 **as**  **is to**

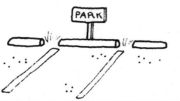 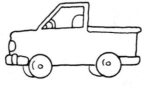 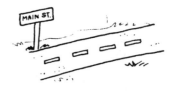

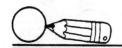

 is to as  is to

 is to  as  is to

 is to as  is to

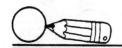

Circle the picture that best completes the sentence.

Circle the picture that best completes the sentence.

 **is to**  **as**  **is to**

 **is to** **8** **as**  **is to**

4   **2**   **6**

 **is to**  **as**  **is to**

Circle the picture that best completes the sentence.

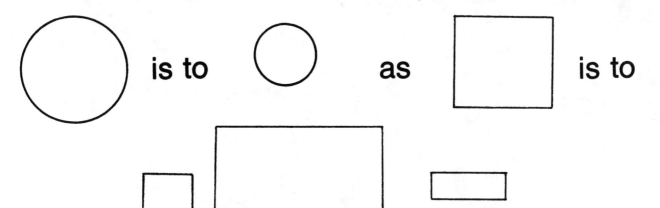

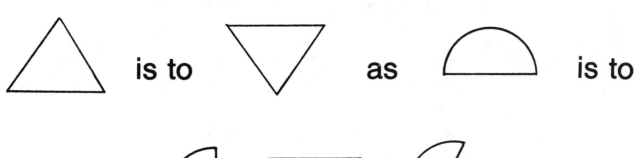

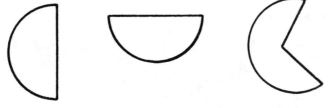

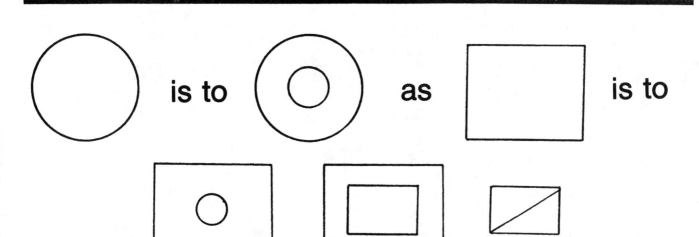

Circle the picture that best completes the sentence.

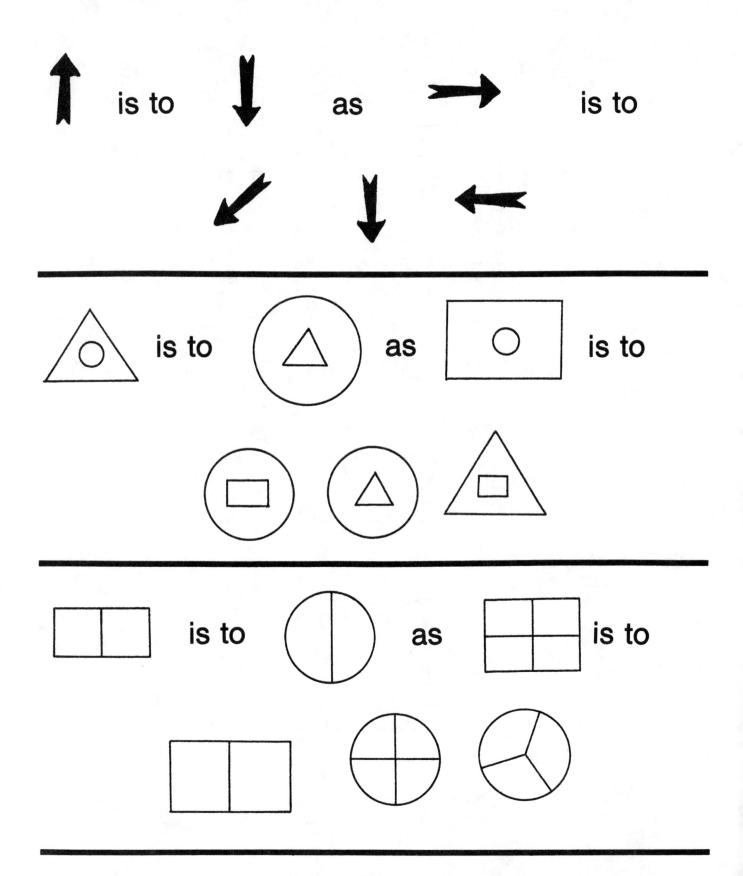

Look at the pictures and the words. Take your time. When you think you can remember them all, turn to the back of this page.

car

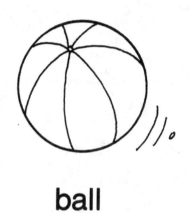

ball

toy

house

Find the words and pictures you saw on the page before. Circle them.

toy

hat

house

rat

car

ball

boat

cat

Look at the words, one at a time. When you think you can remember them all, turn to the back of this page.

car   toy

house   ball

**Find the words you saw on the page before.
Circle only the words you saw before.**

my	go	toy
house	up	look
car	ball	see

MM-EC/1096-9/PB909